Trains Coloring Book

A Color Therapy Book Of Steam Engines, Electric Trains, Trams, Trains & All Things Railroad

Trevor Gordon

ISBN: 9781798873328

INTRODUCTION

All aboard! The railway has always been a source of fascination for so many people. Trains have played a big part in the development of the world as they have allowed for ease of transporting both materials and humans. This train themed color therapy book is designed relieve your mind of stress, anxiety and depression and get it back on track! Next stop a relaxed and happy future! This train focused coloring book is made up for 15 professionally designed images that any railfan, rail buff, train buff, train spotter or anorak would enjoy. While the intricate designs within this coloring book are aimed at adult railway enthusiasts it is also perfect for younger train fans.

A love of the railway can be found in all types of people! Trains are for everyone! Trains are for 3 year old boys and 3 year old girls! Trains are for toddlers, trains are for kids, trains are for adults!

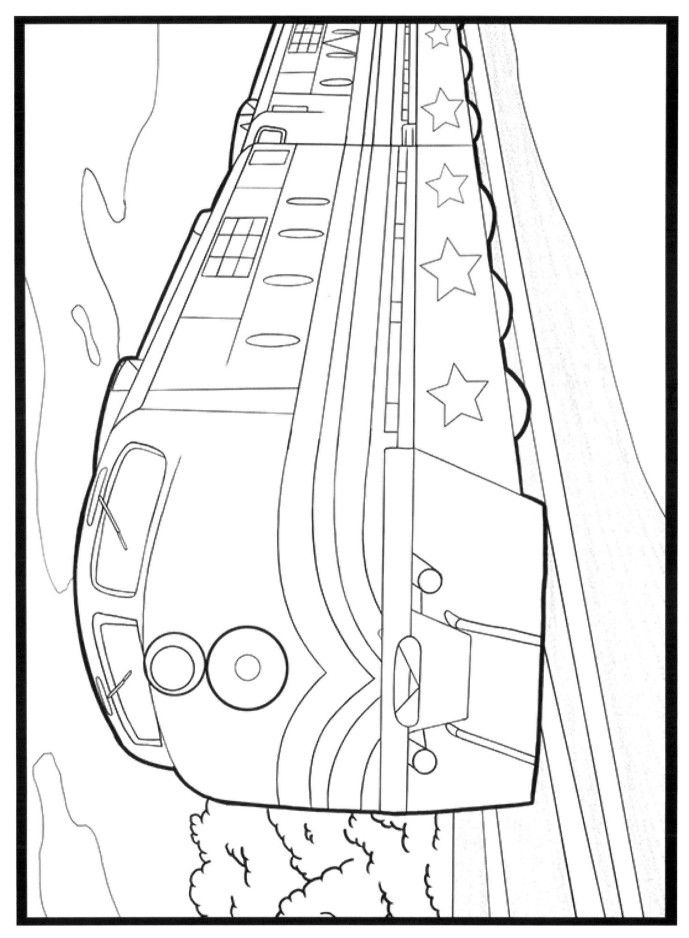

Bleed Page

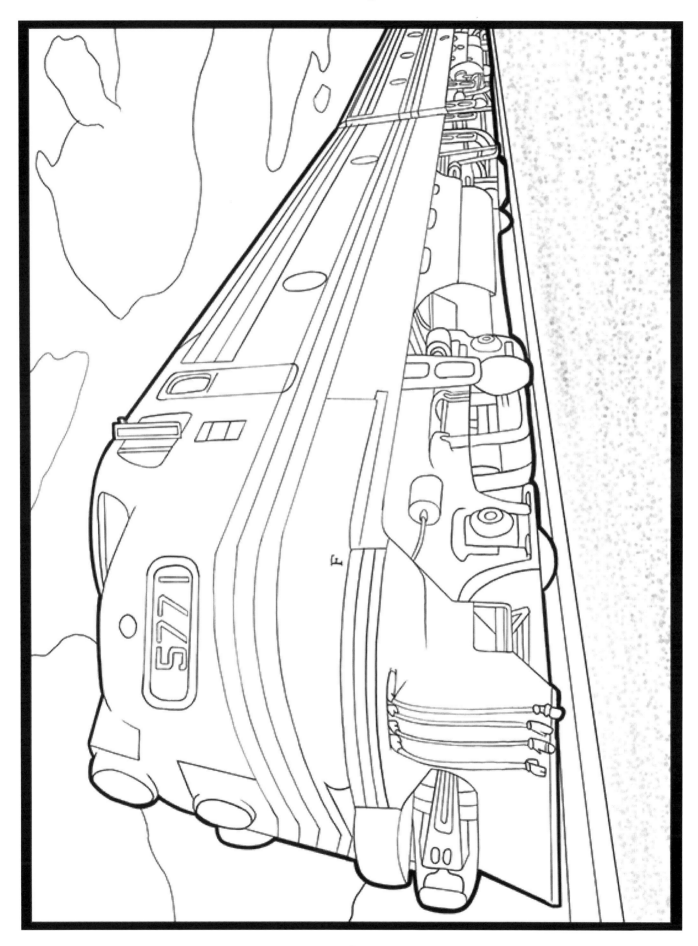

Bleed Page

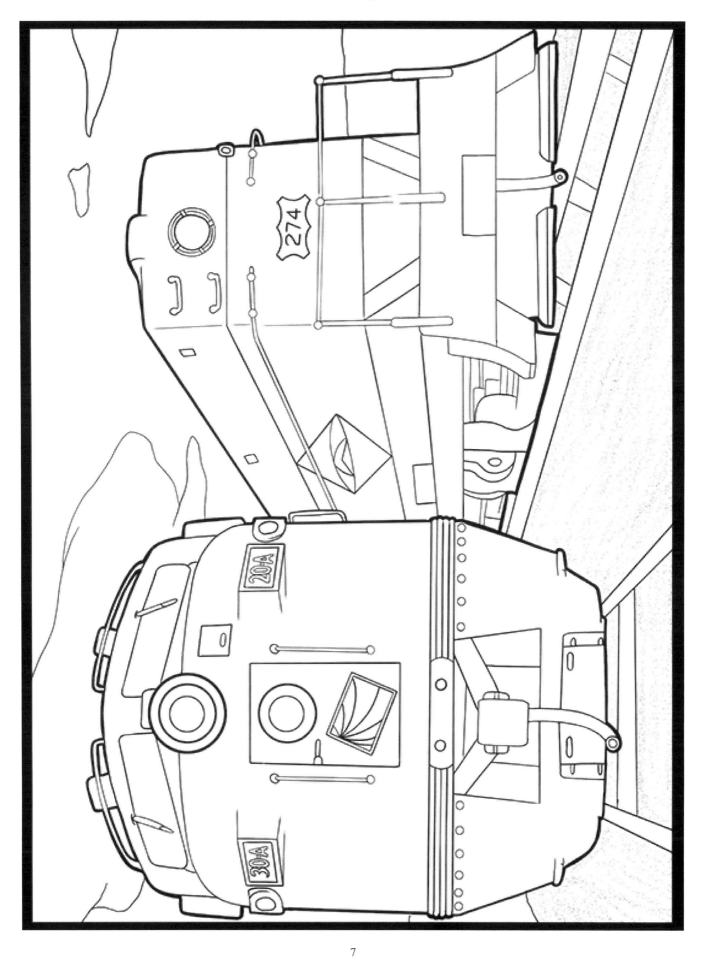

Bleed Page

Bleed Page

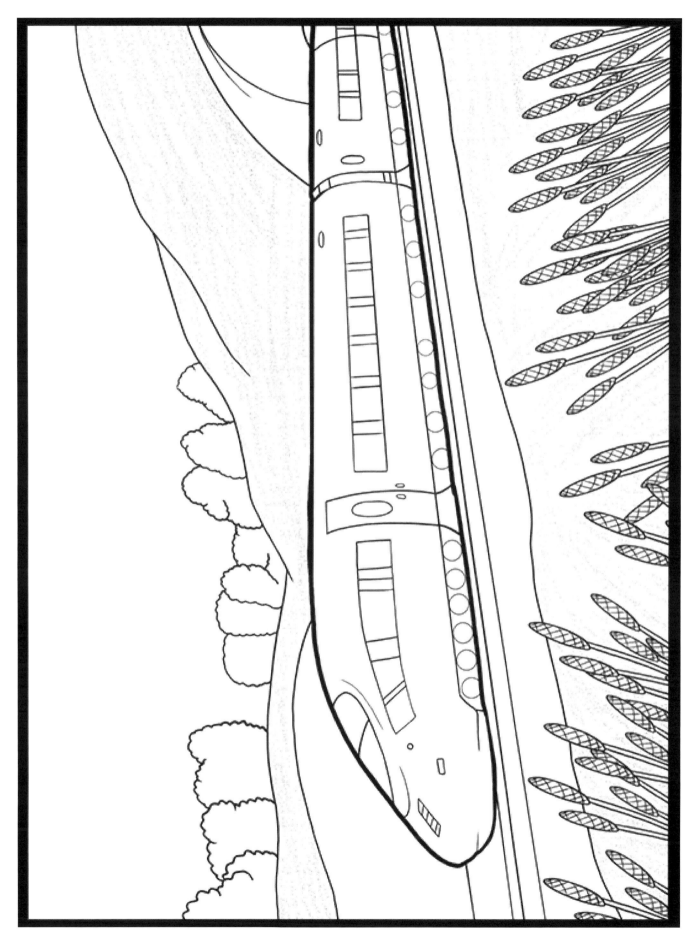

Bleed Page

Bleed Page

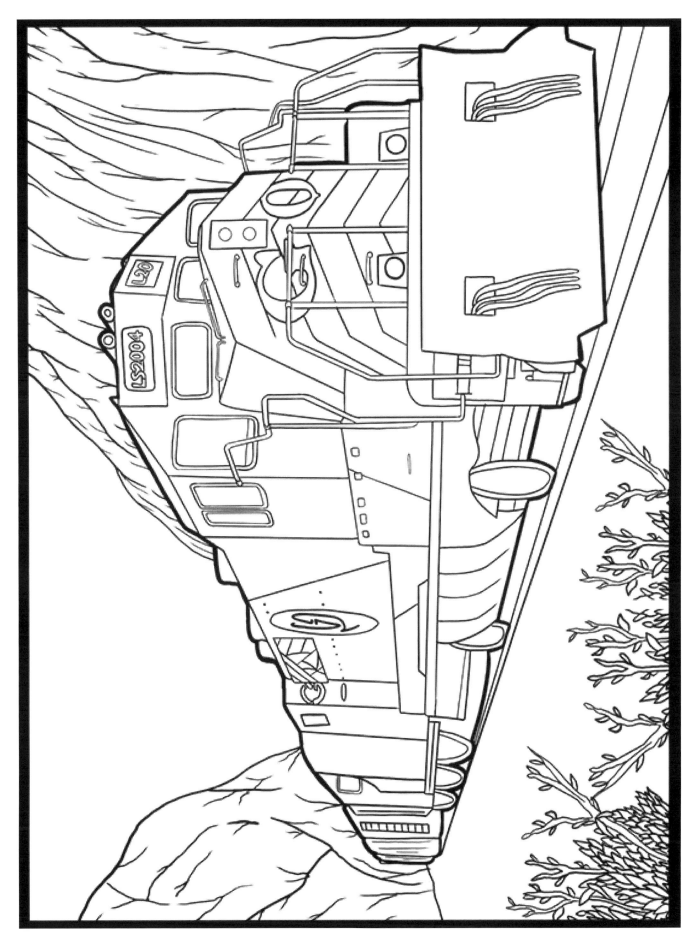

Bleed Page

Bleed Page

Bleed Page

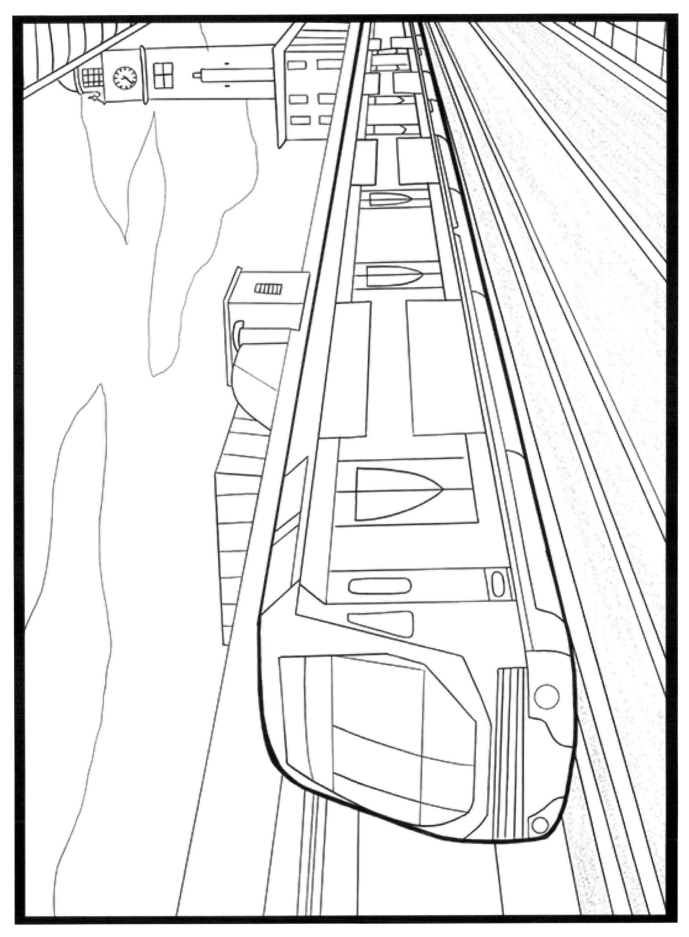

Bleed Page

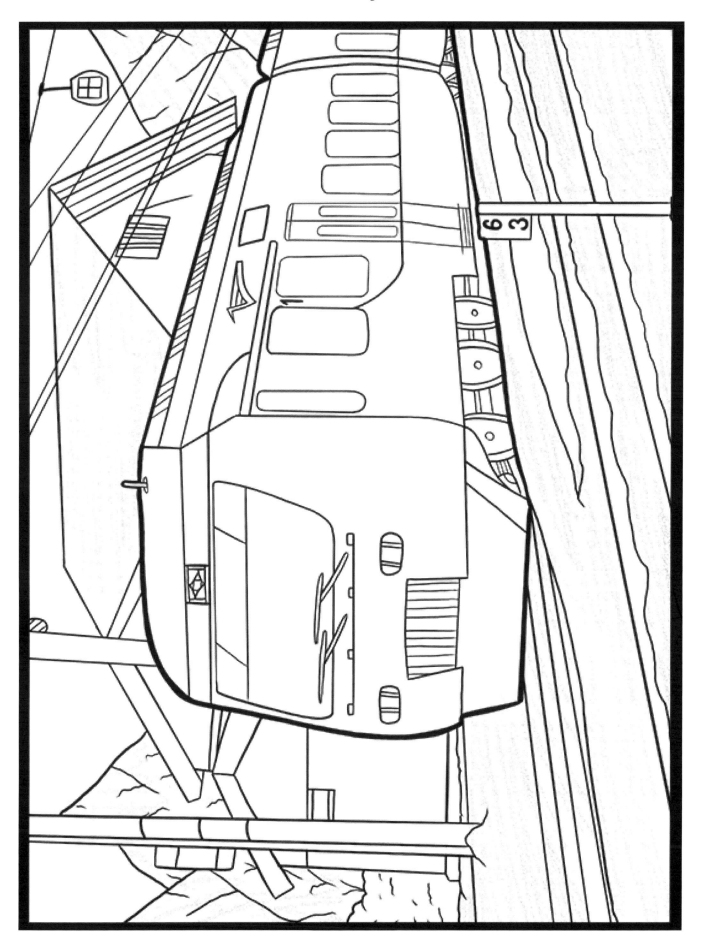

Bleed Page

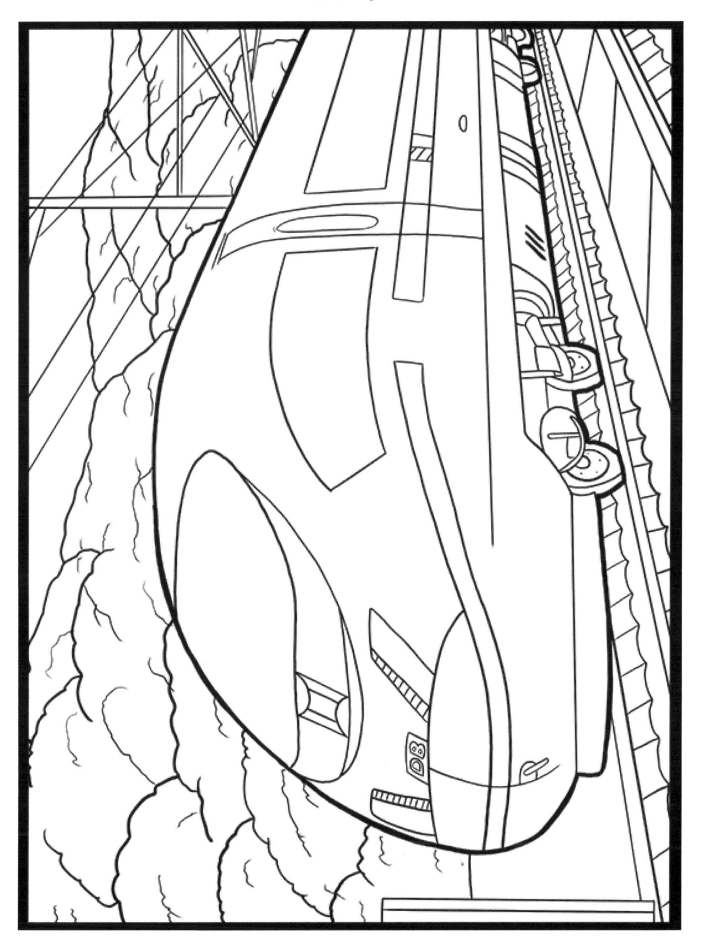

Bleed Page

Bleed Page

Bleed Page

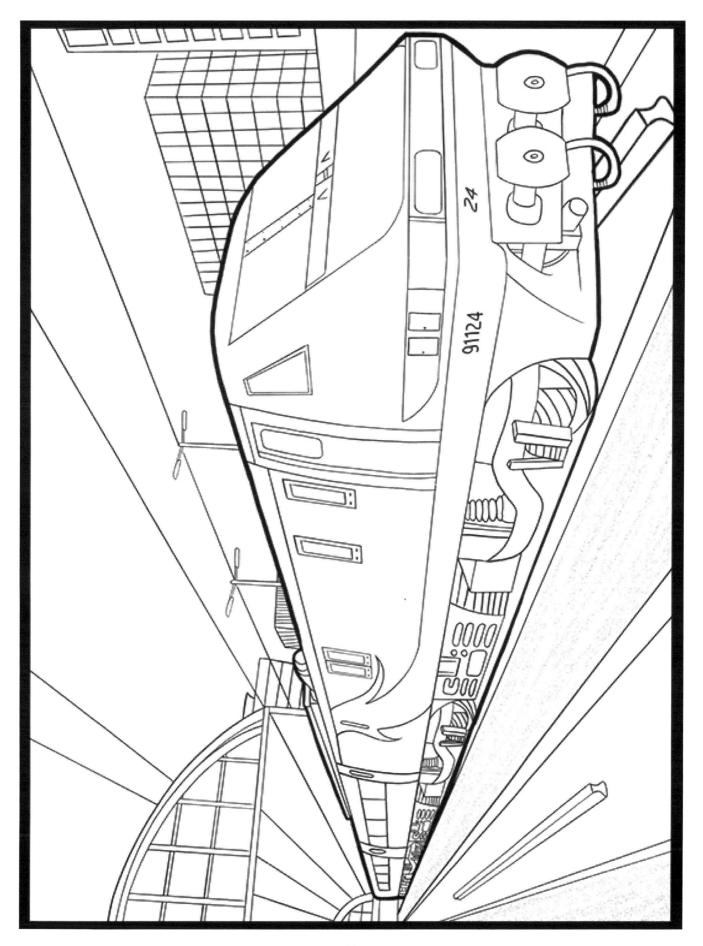

Bleed Page

Colour Test Page

Colour Test Page

Colour Test Page

Printed in Great Britain
by Amazon

82059867R00023